Climate
Change

Eve Hartman and Wendy Meshbesher

Chicago, Illinois

www.heinemannraintree.com
Visit our website to find out more information about Heinemann-Raintree books.

To order:
☎ Phone 888-454-2279
🖥 Visit www.heinemannraintree.com to browse our catalog and order online.

©2010 Raintree
an imprint of Capstone Global Library, LLC
Chicago, Illinois

Edited by Sabrina Crewe
Designed by Sabine Beaupré
Original illustrations © Discovery Books 2009
Illustrated by Stefan Chabluk
Picture research by Sabrina Crewe
Originated by Discovery Books
Printed and bound in China by CTPS

14 13 12 11 10
10 9 8 7 6 5 4 3 2
ISBN 13: 978 1 4109 3352 2 (hardback)

Library of Congress Cataloging-in-Publication Data
Hartman, Eve.
  Climate change / Eve Hartman and Wendy Meshbesher.
     p. cm. -- (Sci-hi. Earth and space science)
  Includes bibliographical references and index.
  ISBN 978-1-4109-3352-2 (hc) -- ISBN 978-1-4109-3362-1 (pb) 1. Climatic changes--Juvenile literature. 2. Climatic changes--Environmental aspects--Juvenile literature. I. Meshbesher, Wendy. II. Title.
  QC903.15.H37 2008
  551.6--dc22
                        2009003538

Acknowledgments
The author and publishers are grateful to the following for permission to reproduce copyright material: © ARUP p. **41**; © FEMA p. **8**; © Getty Images p. **9** (Ian Waldie); © iStockphoto cover inset, pp. **32** (Otmar Smit), **38** bottom right; © Library of Congress p. **42**; © NASA pp. **11**, **15** both; © National Snow and Ice Data Center p. **12**; © NOAA pp. **13**, **26** both, **29**; © Practical Action p. **28** (Kudzai Marovanidze); © Shutterstock pp. **3** top (Sam DCruz), **6** (Steven Vona), **10** (Sam DCruz), **18** (Jessica Bethke), **20** (Tony Strong), **21** (Pavel Cheiko), **22–23** (George Burba), **28** (Steven Vona), **31** (Salamanderman), **34** (JustASC), **36–37** (David P. Lewis), **38** top right & bottom left, **39** both, **43** (JoLin); © U.S. Fish and Wildlife pp. **3** bottom, **40**; © University of Washington Polar Science Center/NOAA p. **5** (Ian Joughin); © Vattenfal p. **17**; © Verdant Power p.**35**; © USDA p. **33** (Keith Weller).

Cover photograph of flood victims in Tangerang, Indonesia, in 2007 is reproduced with permission of Getty Images (Adek Berry/AFP).

We would like to thank content consultant Suzy Gazlay and text consultant Nancy Harris for their invaluable help in the preparation of this book.

Contents

Do volcanoes cause climate change? Go to page 10 to find out.

How does climate change affect animals? Find out on page 40!

Some words are shown in bold, **like this**. These words are explained in the glossary. You will find important information and definitions underlined, **__like this__**.

Evidence of Change

How do we really know that climate change is taking place? When scientists are looking for the truth, they use **evidence**, or visible signs that prove an idea is true. Evidence for climate change comes from decades of weather data, studies of ice, and other observations.

Average and extreme temperatures

Since 1970, Earth's average surface temperatures have risen by about 0.6°C (1°F). A rise of less than one degree may not seem like much, but this is just the rise in **average** temperature. In many places, the hottest days of the year have been hotter than usual. All of the hottest years on record have been very recent. 2005 was the warmest year since world records began in the late 19th century. The second warmest was 1998.

Spotlight on a city: Philadelphia, Pennsylvania

Philadelphia, Pennsylvania, is a large city in the northeastern United States. Over the past thirty years, the average temperature in Philadelphia has been rising. On September 4, 2008, the temperature in Philadelphia reached 34°C (93.2°F), a record high for the date. Winter weather in Philadelphia has been warmer, too.

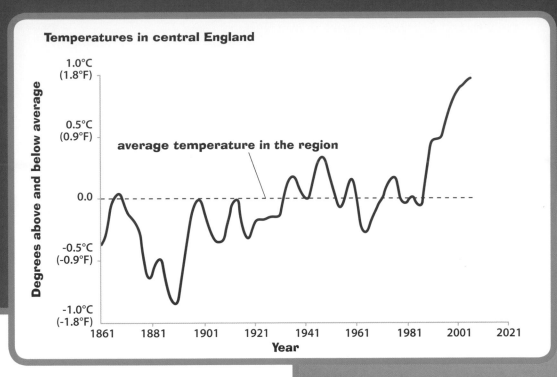

Temperatures in central England

Spotlight on a region: central England

In an area of central England, temperatures have been recorded since 1659. It is the world's longest record, and so it is very useful data for all scientists studying climate change. To prepare the above graph, scientists took an average temperature in the region (the line 0.0). They based the average on a 30-year period. Then they compared temperatures from 1861 to 2005 to that average. The graph shows that average temperatures in central England have risen in recent years to about 1°C (1.8°F) above normal.

Try it: climate survey

What was the climate like thirty, forty, or fifty years ago? Discuss these questions with grandparents or other adults you know. Encourage them to tell stories about the weather, and then compare their stories to your own.

More hurricanes

The huge storms that we know as **hurricanes** form over warm ocean waters. They bring with them dangerously strong winds and heavy rainfall. **Evidence suggests that hurricanes are becoming more frequent and powerful.** In 2004, five hurricanes struck Florida. It was a record number. In 2005, more hurricanes formed in the Atlantic Ocean than in any year before.

El Niño

Most years, the winds blow westward across a **tropical** region of the Pacific Ocean. They help make the surface temperature several degrees cooler off South America than in the western Pacific. In some years, however, these winds reverse direction. They bring warm waters toward South America instead of away from it. This reversal is called *El Niño*. An *El Niño* year is often followed by a pattern called *La Niña*. *La Niña* brings cool waters farther westward than usual.

Hurricane Katrina struck the United States in 2005. Many people lost their homes because of flooding and other damage.

Many names

Hurricane, typhoon, and tropical cyclone are different names for the same type of severe storm. The term used depends on where the storm occurs.

During an *El Niño* event, temperature and rainfall patterns change on both sides of the Pacific Ocean. Rainstorms and floods are frequent along the South American coast. Meanwhile, **droughts** (severe shortages of rainfall) strike Australia and areas of Asia along the Pacific coast.

Before the 1970s, *El Niño* occurred every three to seven years. **Over the past 30 years, *El Niño* events have become more frequent.**

Keeping track

Who keeps track of climate change? **Geophysicists** are the scientists who study Earth's features and environment. They may locate oil or study earthquakes. One field of geophysics is **meteorology**, or the study of climate, weather, and **Earth's atmosphere.**

El Niño events worsen the effects of global warming for farmers and ranchers in Australia. This reservoir dried up completely in 2005.

The debate: natural cycle or global warming?

Some scientists say that more frequent hurricanes and *El Niño* events are parts of Earth's long-term patterns. Others believe that **global warming** is the cause of one or both. They argue that rising ocean temperatures are producing more hurricanes and *El Niño* events.

Change in the Past

FOSSIL CLUES

Fossils of ferns have been found in the icy continent of Antarctica. It is too cold there now for any plants to grow. They show how Earth's surface and climate have changed over time.

Scientists estimate the age of Earth to be about 4.5 billion years. <u>Earth's climate has warmed and cooled many times during its long history</u>. Studies of rocks, fossils, and ice have all provided evidence for these changes.

Volcanic eruptions can cause the climate to change. Gases and ash in the atmosphere block out sunlight, and Earth's surface cools.

Asteroid strike

Earth's climate was hot and humid during the 180 million years when dinosaurs flourished. Some scientists believe dinosaurs and other animals died out after an asteroid like this one (right) struck Earth 65 million years ago. Dust and water vapor blocked out sunlight, and the planet cooled. Many living things could not survive in the new climate.

Changes on Earth

For most of Earth's history, temperatures were warmer than they are today. More recently, Earth has had periods of very cold temperatures. An ice age is usually defined as a lengthy period during which large areas of ice cover much of Earth's surface. Earth has had many ice ages.

Causes of climate change

There are several reasons why Earth's climate has changed so often. One cause is a change in the gases that make up the atmosphere, or blanket of air that surrounds Earth. Another cause is the gradual changing of Earth's surface. Over millions of years, Earth's continents and oceans change shape, size, and position.

A different cause of climate change could be a dramatic, sudden event. One example would be if a giant asteroid, or lump of space rock, hit Earth. Another would be an unusually huge eruption from a volcano. In both cases, gases released into the atmosphere could change the climate.

Melting ice

The melting ice at the North and South poles in recent years is powerful evidence of Earth's rising temperatures. This melting has caused several changes:

Shrinking ice cap

Scientists began measuring the extent of the summer **ice cap** (permanent area of ice) in the Arctic in 1979. Records show that the ice cap is shrinking by about 8 percent a year.

Cracking ice sheets

In both the Arctic and Antarctic ice caps, huge sheets of ice are cracking and breaking apart. In 2008, a section of ice seven times larger than the island of Manhattan in New York City broke apart from Antarctica.

Melting glaciers

A **glacier** is a large piece of ice that moves slowly over land. The world's glaciers are melting at rates faster than before. Glacier National Park in Montana opened in 1910 with more than 100 glaciers. Now there are only 35.

2005

2007

In 2007, the extent of ice in the Arctic Ocean in summer was lower than ever recorded before. These images show how the extent of ice in 2005 compared to 2007. The pink line shows the more usual extent of the ice before 2000.

Ice core studies

In Earth's coldest places, layers of ice and snow build up over many years. An **ice core** is a sample taken from these layers. Scientists collect the sample by drilling a deep hole through the ice.

By looking at ice **molecules** under a microscope, scientists can tell how cold the air was when the ice formed. They can tell when it formed by lines in the ice. **Studies of ice cores confirm that Earth's climate is changing**. Along with ice, each layer contains dust, gases, and other clues to Earth's atmosphere. The clues are all preserved from when the ice formed.

One scientist is drilling for an ice core while another is measuring a core already brought to the surface. Ice cores act as records of Earth's climate over thousands of years. They show many periods of warming and cooling.

The Greenhouse Effect

Scientists agree that Earth's **average** temperatures are rising and its **climate** is changing. What is causing these changes? <u>Most geophysicists say that today's climate change is caused by increasing levels of certain gases in Earth's atmosphere</u>. These gases are part of the greenhouse effect, a process that warms Earth's surface.

Sunlight warms Earth's surface

Some heat escapes

Greenhouse gases trap heat

Trapped heat warms Earth

Greenhouse gases in the atmosphere trap heat and keep Earth warm.

Most common greenhouse gases

1. water vapor
2. carbon dioxide
3. methane
4. nitrous oxide
5. ozone
6. CFCs

What is the greenhouse effect?

A greenhouse is a building lined with windows. The windows allow sunlight to enter, and they trap heat inside. The warmth makes greenhouses ideal for raising plants.

In some ways, certain gases in Earth's **atmosphere** act like a greenhouse. Sunlight travels through the atmosphere and warms Earth's surface. The surface radiates (sends rays of) heat back into the atmosphere. But the gases do not let all this heat energy pass through. The heat is trapped in the atmosphere, making Earth much warmer than it would be otherwise. The gases that trap heat are called **greenhouse gases**. By far the most common greenhouse gas is water vapor. It creates most of the greenhouse effect. Without the greenhouse effect, living things would die.

Getting rid of CFCs

Chlorofluorocarbons (CFCs) are human-made substances. They were useful for refrigerator cooling systems and spray cans. But CFCs were banned around the world in 1987 because they were destroying the ozone layer. Ozone is a harmful greenhouse gas at Earth's surface, but it is important in Earth's upper atmosphere. It protects people and other living things from harmful rays. The use of CFCs has decreased, and the ozone layer is recovering slowly.

Venus

Mercury and Venus

The greenhouse effect works on other planets, not just Earth. Venus has a thick atmosphere that is mostly carbon dioxide. As a result, its surface temperatures are extremely hot. Mercury has a very thin atmosphere. Even though it is much closer to the Sun, Mercury has a colder climate than Venus.

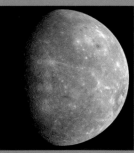

Mercury

The rise of carbon dioxide

Nearly 99 percent of Earth's atmosphere is made of two gases: nitrogen and oxygen. Among the remaining 1 percent, only a tiny fraction is carbon dioxide. Yet this fraction has been changing dramatically.

The amount of carbon dioxide in Earth's atmosphere has been rising for more than one hundred years. It has risen by about 35 percent since the mid-1800s. The rate of the rise has been steadily speeding up.

What caused the rise?

Fossil fuels are the energy-rich remains of ancient plants and animals. These fuels include coal, oil, and natural gas. They are burned for energy in **power plants**, automobiles, and other devices. The burning releases carbon dioxide as a waste gas.

Scientists believe that levels of carbon dioxide in the air have increased due to this burning of fossil fuels. In the middle of the 19th century, people began mining and burning fossil fuels in large amounts. This is about the same time that carbon dioxide levels began to rise.

Carbon dioxide levels in the atmosphere have increased for other reasons, too. Trees store vast amounts of carbon. Like fossil fuels, wood releases carbon dioxide when it is burned. Many forests have been cut down to clear land for farming. Much of the wood is burned, releasing carbon dioxide into the air.

What is carbon dioxide?

Carbon dioxide is made of carbon and oxygen. In the air, it's a gas. As a solid, it forms dry ice and is used to keep things cold. As a liquid, it is used in fire extinguishers.

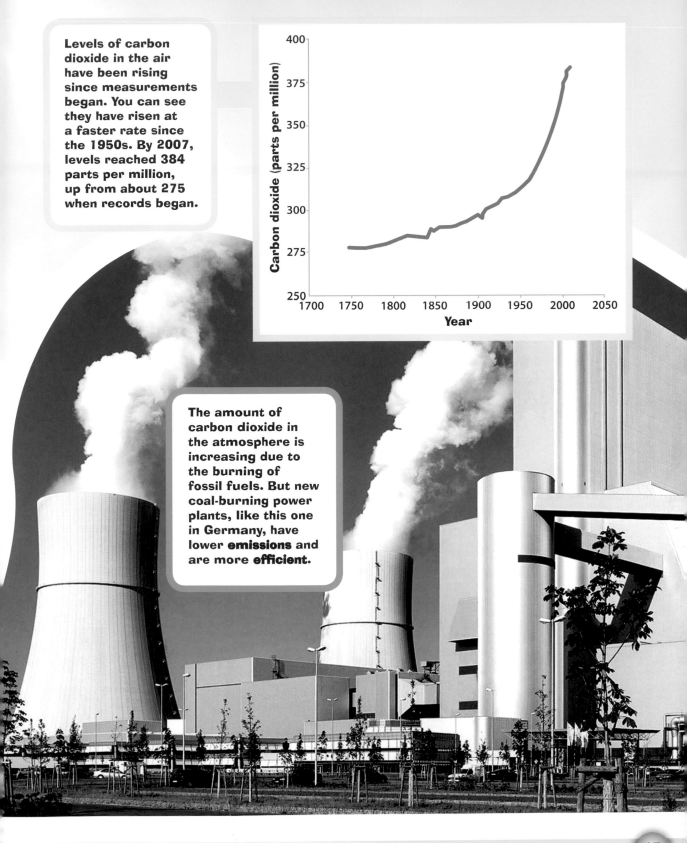

Levels of carbon dioxide in the air have been rising since measurements began. You can see they have risen at a faster rate since the 1950s. By 2007, levels reached 384 parts per million, up from about 275 when records began.

The amount of carbon dioxide in the atmosphere is increasing due to the burning of fossil fuels. But new coal-burning power plants, like this one in Germany, have lower **emissions** and are more **efficient**.

THE CARBON CYCLE

Carbon is an **element** (a substance made of a single type of **atom**). It is not especially common either on Earth's surface or in its **atmosphere**. Yet carbon is available to all of Earth's living things. The reason is that carbon reacts with other elements to form a wide variety of **compounds** (combinations of elements). These compounds can be solids, liquids, or gases.

<u>As Earth's carbon changes from one compound to another, it moves between the surface and atmosphere</u>. This movement is called the **carbon cycle**. A cycle is something that continues to happen in the same order.

Tons of carbon

Scientists measure carbon dioxide **emissions** by the weight of the carbon they contain. The burning of fossil fuels and other human-caused processes places about 7.2 billion metric tons (7.9 billion tons) of carbon into the atmosphere each year.

During photosynthesis, plants and algae absorb carbon dioxide and release oxygen. We can show this as: water and carbon dioxide → glucose and oxygen, or:
$$6H_2O + 6CO_2 \rightarrow C_6H_{12}O_6 + 6O_2$$

Life and the carbon cycle

Every living thing on Earth plays a part in the carbon cycle. The process that takes **carbon dioxide** from the atmosphere is called **photosynthesis**. During the process, plants and **algae** (simple plantlike life forms) take in carbon dioxide from the air. They use photosynthesis to make glucose (a type of sugar), which they need to survive and grow. The process produces oxygen.

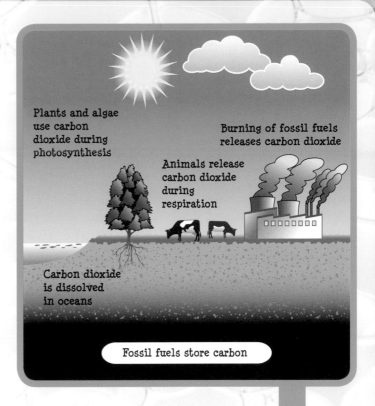

Plants and algae use carbon dioxide during photosynthesis

Burning of fossil fuels releases carbon dioxide

Animals release carbon dioxide during respiration

Carbon dioxide is dissolved in oceans

Fossil fuels store carbon

Living things also perform the reverse process, which is **respiration**. In respiration, the carbon compounds of living things are broken apart. All animals—including humans—perform respiration to get energy from the food they eat. The process produces carbon dioxide.

This diagram shows how carbon moves from Earth's land and water into the atmosphere.

Tipping the balance

For most of human history, Earth's living things removed carbon dioxide from the atmosphere at about the same rate that they released it. Beginning in the 19th century, however, people began to burn more **fossil fuels** and to use them in factories. They also started using fossil fuels for transportation fuel and to produce electricity.

<u>**Fossil fuels contain carbon taken from the atmosphere millions of years ago**</u>. Today, the burning of fossil fuels is adding that carbon to the atmosphere faster than natural processes can remove it. The carbon cycle cannot remove all the carbon produced today.

Carbon sinks

A carbon sink is a storehouse. It takes in and stores carbon dioxide from the atmosphere. Plants and algae act as **carbon sinks**. They take in carbon dioxide during photosynthesis. Earth's largest carbon sinks, however, are its oceans.

Carbon dioxide dissolves in ocean water. **Scientists estimate that oceans are dissolving up to one-third of the extra carbon dioxide being added to the atmosphere**. Unfortunately, ocean waters may become saturated (full) with carbon dioxide. If the oceans become saturated, then the amount of carbon dioxide in the atmosphere will rise even faster.

Ocean life forms

Algae and other ocean organisms (living things) take in carbon dioxide as they perform photosynthesis. About 80 percent of all photosynthesis on Earth takes place in the oceans. Together, ocean life forms make up a huge carbon sink.

Many organisms in the ocean use carbon dioxide to make shells and other hard body parts. When these organisms die and sink to the bottom, their shells may become pressed into rocks. Limestone is one type of rock that forms this way.

Seaweed and other algae absorb huge amounts of carbon dioxide during photosynthesis. The oceans and the living things within them are important carbon sinks.

Forests and soil

All growing plants take in carbon dioxide from the atmosphere. Therefore they all act as carbon sinks. A forest of tall trees holds much more carbon than that same area of wheat or other crops. Soil also holds carbon, much of it as decaying plant matter. Some scientists believe that soil stores more carbon than all plants and the atmosphere combined.

Soil solution?

Some scientists think we can use carbon sinks on land and in the oceans to help solve **global warming**. David Manning, Professor of Soil Science at Newcastle University in Britain, is designing a special soil to do the job. It will store carbon permanently by mixing it with calcium.

The pine trees of Canada hold great stores of carbon. Even more carbon is held in the soil beneath them.

A FROZEN CARBON SINK

Siberia is a freezing cold region of northern Asia. It is huge, covering about 10 percent of all Earth's land. In this cold expanse, the soil just below the surface can stay frozen all year long. This type of soil is called permafrost. In some parts of Siberia, the permafrost is nearly 1,500 meters (4,200 feet) deep!

Siberian permafrost

Like other soils, permafrost acts as a carbon sink. But **because of global warming, the Siberian permafrost is now melting. This leads to the release of some of the carbon it holds.** Scientists are concerned that melting permafrost could speed up **climate** change. they are especially worried about the melting of a type of permafrost called **yedoma**. Yedoma covers more than 1 million square kilometers (386,000 square miles) in northeast Siberia.

The carbon bomb

Yedoma is very rich in carbon. Altogether, the yedoma of Siberia may hold 500 billion metric tons (550 billion tons) of carbon. When yedoma melts, **bacteria** and other microorganisms (microscopic living things) start acting on remains of plants and animals in the soil. The remains begin to decay, or rot. This decay releases both carbon dioxide and heat. The heat melts the yedoma further and promotes more decay. The process speeds up as more heat is released.

<u>Once the melting of the yedoma reaches a certain level, it will continue until all of its stored carbon is released</u>. This dumping of carbon could take as little as 100 years to complete. For this reason, scientists describe the yedoma as a carbon bomb. Earth's rising temperatures could easily "light the fuse" and release the yedoma carbon into the atmosphere.

This map shows parts of Siberia and other lands around the Arctic Ocean. The orange areas show the places where the permafrost usually stays frozen all year round.

NORTH AMERICA

Arctic Ocean

Siberia

North Pole

ASIA

EUROPE

THE OCEAN AND CLIMATE CHANGE

Whether you live near or far from the ocean shore, the ocean affects your climate. **Evaporation is the process of liquid turning into gas.** Evaporation from oceans provides most of the **water vapor** in the **atmosphere.** This water vapor eventually falls as rain or snow. Oceans also affect the temperature of nearby land as well as wind patterns and storms.

As Earth's **average** temperatures rise, oceans could affect the global climate in several ways. Scientists continue to study and raise concerns about these potential changes.

Ocean currents

At certain depths, ocean waters flow in specific patterns called **currents**. You can think of an ocean current as a river of water flowing within the ocean.

Ocean currents form for many reasons, including differences in water temperature.

The Gulf Stream

One of the strongest and most important ocean currents is the Gulf Stream. This current carries warm water from the Gulf of Mexico to the northeastern Atlantic Ocean. Without this warmth, northern Europe would have a much colder, harsher climate than it has today.

Some currents carry warm water from the **tropical** regions. Other currents carry cold water from the North and South poles.

Ocean currents help to even out the temperature differences between Earth's cold poles and warm tropics. They greatly affect climates in all regions of the world. The map above shows some the world's main currents.

Currents and climate change

Scientists are concerned that if global temperatures continue rising, ocean currents could weaken, change, or disappear. **Changes to ocean currents would make some lands hotter and others colder. They also would change other climate patterns.** The effects of *El Niño*, described on page 8, show how ocean currents can affect climate.

Rising ocean levels

The water level of Earth's oceans has risen and fallen many times during the past. Scientists have found **evidence** of human **civilizations** in areas now covered by ocean waters.

Ocean levels fall during ice ages. During these periods, a huge volume of water is trapped on land in **glaciers** and ice sheets. Levels rise when this land ice melts. Because of **global warming**, some scientists predict that **ocean levels may rise at least 1 meter (3 feet) by the year 2100**. Oceans could rise even more in the years that follow.

Scientists estimate that for every 1-meter (3-foot) rise of ocean waters, coastlines would retreat by about 1,500 meters (about 1 mile). By 2100, coastal regions could face frequent or permanent flooding. These regions include some of the world's major cities. Ocean water could completely cover some island nations, such as the Maldives in the Indian Ocean.

Global warming is changing the temperatures, currents, levels, and salinity (saltiness) of oceans. All these changes threaten marine life.

CORAL REEFS

Coral reefs are hard structures made up of living organisms. Healthy reefs (left) are home to many ocean life forms. Over the past twenty years, coral reefs such as this one (right) have been dying in tropical ocean waters all over the world. Scientists suspect that a rise in ocean temperature is one cause.

Ice melt

EXpaNdiNg Water

Water expands (gets bigger) as it gets warmer. This expansion adds to the rise of sea levels during global warming.

If ice melts in the ocean, how does it change the level of ocean water? What if ice on land melts, as glaciers are doing? Experiment on a model of Earth to find out.

You will need:

- a plastic food container
- modeling clay
- water
- ice cubes

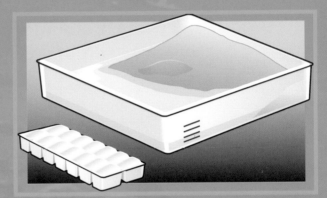

1. In the food container, mold the modeling clay into a shape to represent land. Add water to represent the ocean.

2. Place some ice cubes in the ocean. Measure and record the water level. Let the ice melt, and observe the water level to see if it has changed.

3. Start over, but place the ice cubes on the land instead of in the ocean. Measure and record the water level. Then let the ice melt, and observe the water level to see if it has changed.

4. Compare the results.

The Effect on Plants and Animals

All plants and animals have their own particular **habitat**, or home, in which they thrive. **Climate change is affecting habitats all over Earth. The change threatens a large number of plants and animals**. Some scientists say **climate** change is the biggest threat to wildlife today.

Farming in a warming world

Like other plants, farm crops depend on the weather to grow and thrive. **Climate change affects the food supply worldwide**. **Droughts** and floods can damage crops.

Farmers can help combat climate change, however. **Sustainable** agriculture is farming that meets the need for food while not causing damage or using up resources. Farmers can use irrigation (watering) methods that make better use of water. They can grow drought-resistant crops, which are plants that cope with dry conditions. Sustainable farming methods also include keeping the soil healthy. These factors can help a tiny farm in Africa that supports one family. They are just as important to huge farms in **industrialized nations**, where there are many industries and high energy use.

Conserving water is an important part of sustainable farming. These farmers use a water-saving system called drip irrigation. It drips water from a hose into the soil around the plants.

Spotlight on a species:
penguins

Many penguins gather in Antarctica every summer. They raise their chicks on the icy land, and they fish in the cold waters. In 2008, heavy rains fell on western Antarctica. It was unusual weather for the region. The rains killed thousands of penguin chicks that had not yet grown feathers that could repel (keep off) water.

Antarctic rain is only one of the ways that **global warming** is threatening penguins. As ice sheets break away from the mainland, they form huge icebergs in the ocean. The changing patterns of ice confuse the penguins as they try to find their breeding grounds. Global warming and lack of ice is also harming fish populations. This affects the penguins' food supply.

Temperatures in parts of Antarctica are rising faster than in other places. Experts from the World Wildlife Fund (WWF) said in 2008 that some kinds of penguins faced **extinction** if the world continues to warm.

Solutions to Climate Change

There is strong **evidence** that **climate** change will continue unless people everywhere address its cause. **Climate change is a global problem that requires global solutions**. Such solutions are possible.

Reducing greenhouse gases

Today, nearly all scientists agree on the basic facts of climate change. **Rising levels of greenhouse gases are changing Earth's climate, oceans, and living things**. They also agree on the response to the problem. Reducing these gases will help slow or undo these changes. The most significant of the **greenhouse gases** is **carbon dioxide**. So, to combat climate change, people are looking for ways of reducing carbon dioxide levels in the **atmosphere**.

Carbon footprints

Like other animals, humans release carbon dioxide when they exhale. But they also release it in other ways. **Fossil fuels** are burned in vehicles, **power plants**, and furnaces. When people use or benefit from these things, they account for some of the carbon dioxide they produce.

Your **carbon footprint** is the amount of carbon dioxide that your actions add to the atmosphere. On **average**, every person on Earth adds about 1.2 metric tons (1.3 tons) of carbon every year. The amount is much higher in **industrialized nations** (nations with a lot of factories and high energy use). It is much lower in countries with fewer industries, or **developing nations**. In the near future, however, these nations will become more industrialized. Their citizens will use more electrical devices and drive more automobiles. Their carbon footprints will therefore get bigger. **To combat climate change, people and nations will need to limit their carbon footprints**.

Callendar's claim

Scientists have been observing Earth's rising temperatures for at least 100 years. As early as 1938, British engineer G. S. Callendar claimed that carbon dioxide was the cause of this rise.

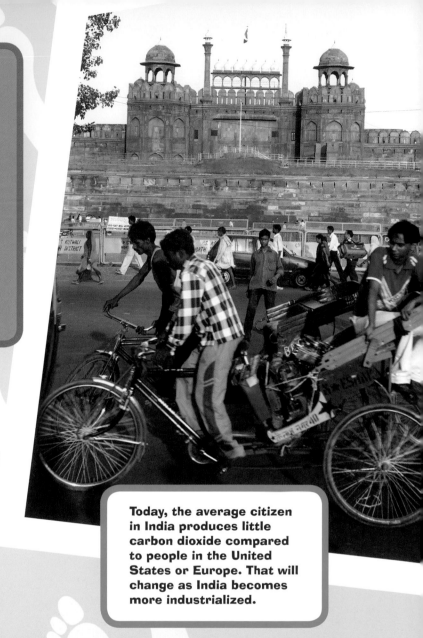

This chart shows the carbon **emissions** (in metric tons) per person in different countries and in the world. You can see how emission levels increased in most places from 1985 to 2005. Developing nations produce much less carbon per person. But overall, China emits more carbon than any other nation because of its huge population.

Today, the average citizen in India produces little carbon dioxide compared to people in the United States or Europe. That will change as India becomes more industrialized.

Carbon emissions

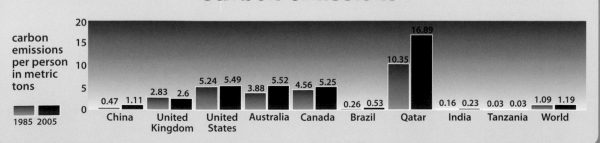

carbon emissions per person in metric tons

1985 2005

	China	United Kingdom	United States	Australia	Canada	Brazil	Qatar	India	Tanzania	World
1985	0.47	2.83	5.24	3.88	4.56	0.26	10.35	0.16	0.03	1.09
2005	1.11	2.6	5.49	5.52	5.25	0.53	16.89	0.23	0.03	1.19

Helpful steps

Global warming would probably slow down if people everywhere stopped burning fossil fuels. Yet people depend on the transportation and electricity that these fuels provide. **Many scientists believe that the world's nations cannot stop global warming in the near future, but they can take steps to slow it down.**

Making changes, solving problems

So how can these changes be made? Who is going to make them? Countries can work together. Governments can pass laws that encourage people to be less wasteful. Businesses can invest in new ideas. Scientists can come up with ways to combat climate change. All of us can make changes to save energy at home. In the next few pages, we will look at the ways people are reducing their carbon footprints. These ways include conserving fossil fuels, developing new energy sources, and planting trees.

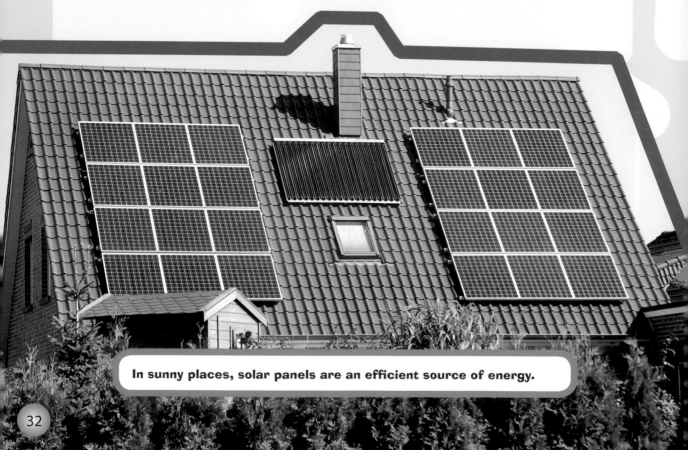

In sunny places, solar panels are an efficient source of energy.

This bus runs on fuel made from soybeans.

Conserving fossil fuels

To conserve means to use wisely. **Efficient** (not wasteful) use of fuel helps save resources. People can conserve fuel by buying fuel-efficient cars and appliances. They can use **mass transit** systems, such as buses and trains, and reduce energy use at home.

Developing alternative energy

Energy can be harnessed from **renewable** sources, which are energy sources that don't run out. These renewable sources include the wind, the sun, moving water, and geothermal energy (underground heat). Scientists are finding ways to make these energy sources more efficient.

Planting trees and saving forests

All plants take up carbon dioxide as they grow. Because of this, the world's forests store great amounts of carbon. But forests are being cut down as people expand farms and cities. We are losing these important **carbon sinks**. People can plant new trees, however. The trees will absorb carbon dioxide from the atmosphere.

Goals for government and industry

In the last few years, governments have been working together to find solutions to climate change. Industries are helping, too. They are developing new products and building cleaner, more efficient factories. The auto industry is making vehicles that run on renewable fuels. The world's governments and businesses are learning that **sustainable** development is important for the planet. It will ensure we that we have resources for the future.

Plastic lumber

More and more businesses are selling products that help conserve fossil fuels. Plastic is made from oil, which is a fossil fuel. Some plastics can be recycled, and businesses are using them to make plastic lumber, a replacement for wood. Not only does it conserve oil supplies and reduce waste, but it saves on wood, too!

A lot of energy is saved by recycling plastic into new products.

International agreements

In the 1990s, the United Nations began efforts to reduce greenhouse gases worldwide. These efforts led to a treaty (agreement) called the Kyoto Protocol. It was named for the city of Kyoto, Japan, where the treaty was proposed. **The Kyoto Protocol required industrialized nations to meet targets for reducing greenhouse gases**. In 2005, nations met in Montreal, Canada, for the largest climate conference ever held. They created the Montreal Action Plan. This agreement extended the Kyoto treaty and created higher targets.

The cost of energy

The decision to conserve energy helps fight global warming. Yet people often make this decision for a different reason: to save money. **The cost of fossil fuels is rising higher than ever before**. As a result, conserving and replacing fossil fuels seems more attractive. The wise choice is also an economical (money-saving) one.

Many people say that governments can reduce the use of fossil fuels by making them cost more. Some suggest higher **taxes** on gasoline. Others say industries adding carbon dioxide to the atmosphere should pay fees.

Energy producers are turning to alternative forms of energy, and governments are supporting them. Wind **turbines** such as this one can produce huge amounts of electricity. Today, 1 percent of the world's electricity comes from wind power, but that figure is growing every year.

Carbon capture and storage

Coal is burned in power plants all over the world. Today, coal accounts for about half of the carbon dioxide released from fossil fuels. Must all that carbon dioxide be released into the atmosphere? Perhaps not! A new method called carbon capture and storage is being tested.

Carbon capture involves taking carbon dioxide from the air and pumping it deep underground. The gas is then stored at least 800 meters (2,600 feet) below the surface. Scientists think that some rock could hold carbon dioxide for thousands, even millions, of years.

In another form of carbon capture, the carbon dioxide from a power plant is mixed with a chemical called sodium hydroxide. This forms a white powdery substance called sodium bicarbonate. The sodium bicarbonate is buried to prevent the release of its carbon into the atmosphere.

New science

Scientists from many fields are studying new ideas for slowing or reversing the effects of global warming. They are developing ways to reduce carbon dioxide emissions from fossil fuels. They are focusing on new forms of energy that are sustainable and do not produce carbon dioxide.

Energy-wise design

Buildings use lots of energy to stay warm in winter and keep cool in summer. Today, scientists and architects are studying ways

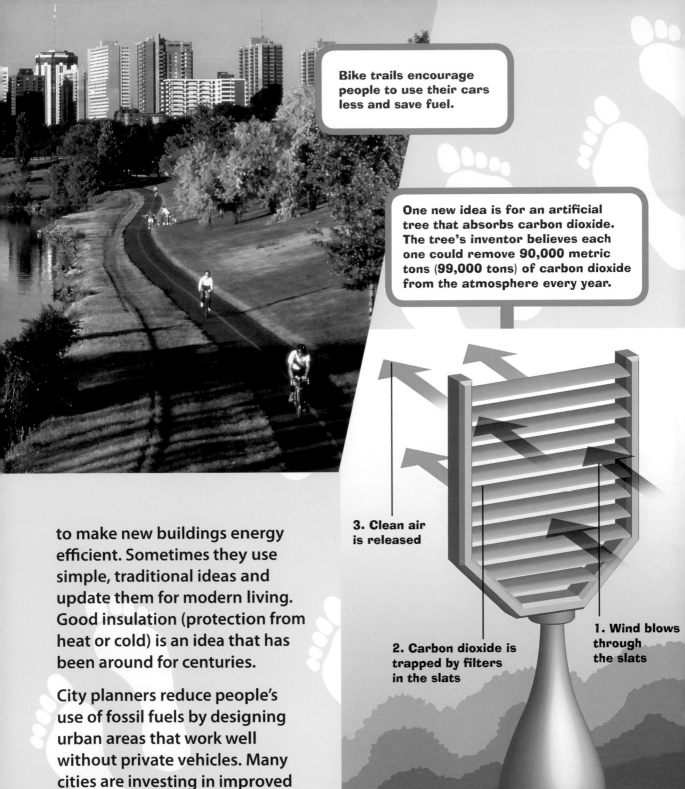

Bike trails encourage people to use their cars less and save fuel.

One new idea is for an artificial tree that absorbs carbon dioxide. The tree's inventor believes each one could remove **90,000 metric tons** (**99,000 tons**) of carbon dioxide from the atmosphere every year.

3. Clean air is released

2. Carbon dioxide is trapped by filters in the slats

1. Wind blows through the slats

to make new buildings energy efficient. Sometimes they use simple, traditional ideas and update them for modern living. Good insulation (protection from heat or cold) is an idea that has been around for centuries.

City planners reduce people's use of fossil fuels by designing urban areas that work well without private vehicles. Many cities are investing in improved mass transit, trails for bicycles, and new housing close to business districts.

Climate Change and You

No one can slow or reverse climate change by themselves. But by working together, people can make a big difference. **You can help fight climate change by being part of the solution**. Here are a few simple steps that you and your friends and family can take.

Park the car

Rather than riding in the family vehicle, you can walk, ride a bike, or use mass transit. The exercise will make you much healthier. When people use the car, they can combine several errands in a single trip.

Don't touch that thermostat

Air conditioning and home heating use huge amounts of energy. Try other ways of managing indoor temperatures. Open a window, put on a sweater, or close off a room that you aren't using.

Replace light bulbs

Compact fluorescent light bulbs use much less energy and last longer than older styles of light bulb. And you can save money, too.

Buy local foods

Most foods are shipped across the country or from overseas. A lot of fossil fuels were burned to bring them to your local store. If you have the choice, choose foods grown locally. It will also support people in your community.

Waste less

- Turn off lights and devices when you are not using them.
- Try not to buy items that have a lot of packaging.
- Don't throw away food or things that you can repair or recycle.

Plant a tree

A tree planted in your street or yard can take up as much carbon dioxide as a tree anywhere else in the world. Trees also provide shade during a hot summer.

Timeline

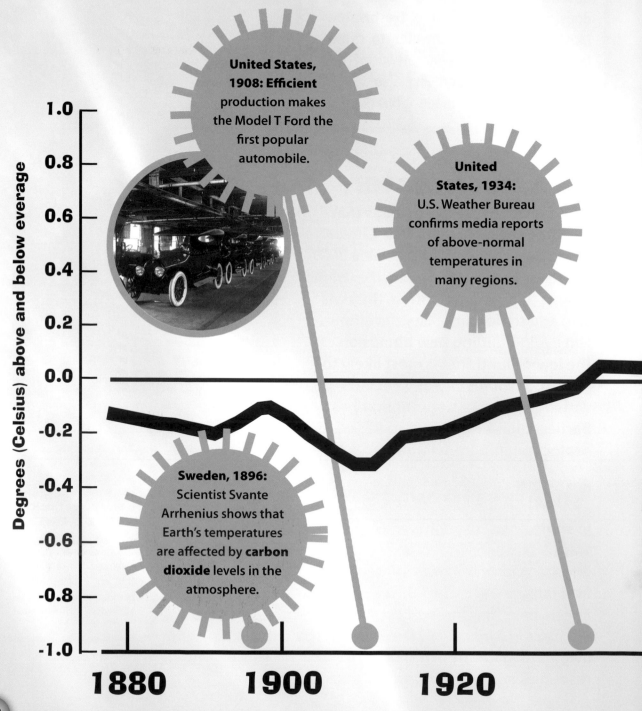

Degrees (Celsius) above and below everage

1.0
0.8
0.6
0.4
0.2
0.0
-0.2
-0.4
-0.6
-0.8
-1.0

United States, 1908: Efficient production makes the Model T Ford the first popular automobile.

United States, 1934: U.S. Weather Bureau confirms media reports of above-normal temperatures in many regions.

Sweden, 1896: Scientist Svante Arrhenius shows that Earth's temperatures are affected by **carbon dioxide** levels in the atmosphere.

1880   1900   1920

This graph shows how much global temperatures for the years 1880–2007 varied from the **average**. The average temperature is the line 0.0. Before 1980, average temperatures were mostly below or around normal. Since then, they have been rising. Since 2000, global temperatures have been about 0.5°C (0.9°F) above the average.

England, 1938: Scientist G. S. Callendar suggests carbon dioxide levels are raising global temperatures.

China, 2007: China replaces United States as Earth's biggest source of carbon **emissions**.

United States, 1958: Scientist David Keeling starts measuring carbon dioxide levels and soon reports a yearly rise.

Japan, 1997: Many nations sign the Kyoto Protocol, a treaty to reduce the world's **greenhouse gas** emissions.

1940   **1960**   **1980**   **2000**

Climate Change Review

- Scientific **evidence** shows that Earth's **average** temperatures have been slowly rising, thus changing the global **climate**.

- Most scientists agree that the main cause of climate change is the burning of **fossil fuels**. These fuels release **greenhouse gases** that trap heat in the **atmosphere**.

- The most significant greenhouse gas is **carbon dioxide**. As levels of carbon dioxide rise, global temperatures rise, too.

- Climate change causes an increase in severe weather patterns. It also can lead to lack of rainfall in some areas and increased rainfall in others. Ocean **currents** are affected, too.

- Scientists predict many consequences of climate change. Among them are rising ocean levels, threatened wildlife, flooding of islands and coastal areas, **drought**, and a shrinking food supply.

- Many nations have set goals to reduce their release of carbon dioxide into the atmosphere.

- Scientists are developing new ideas to combat and adapt to climate change.

- The use of fossil fuels will become cleaner and more **efficient**.

- The use of **renewable** energy sources, such as wind, water, and solar power is increasing. New technology is lowering the cost and increasing the efficiency of renewable sources.

- Everyone can help by reducing their energy use in the home and by planting trees.

Glossary

algae simple, plantlike life forms that live in water and have no roots or seeds

atmosphere layer of gases that surrounds Earth and other planets

atom small piece of matter that everything is made up of

average middle or typical amount or point in a group

bacteria microscopic, single-celled organisms

carbon cycle continual movement of carbon from one form to another and between Earth's surface and atmosphere

carbon dioxide (CO_2) gas composed of carbon and oxygen

carbon footprint amount of carbon that a person's actions add to the atmosphere

carbon sink store of carbon that takes in carbon dioxide from the atmosphere

CFCs human-made compounds that are also greenhouse gases. Their use in products is now banned.

civilization group of people who developed a culture and society in a certain period

climate overall weather patterns of a region over a long time

compound substance made of more than one kind of atom

current pattern of water flowing through the ocean like a river

data sets of information collected over a period of time

developing nation country that is starting to consume more energy and build industries

drought severe and usually longlasting period of little or no rainfall

efficient producing results with little waste of energy

element simple substance made of just one kind of atom

emission substance released into the air, such as gases released by the burning of fossil fuels

evidence visible signs that act as proof of an idea or belief

extinction end of a species

fossil fuels fuels, including coal, natural gas, and petroleum (oil), that contain carbon and were formed underground from plant and animal matter

geophysicist scientist who studies Earth's features and the environment

glacier huge piece of ice on land that is gradually moving, like a very slow river

global warming gradual rise in the average temperature of Earth's surface

greenhouse gas gas in the atmosphere that traps heat

habitat type of place, such as a coral reef or mountain, that is home to a particular group of plants and animals

hurricane powerful storm that forms over the ocean, also known as typhoon or tropical cyclone

ice cap permanent area of ice

ice core sample taken from layers of ice that have formed over centuries. Ice cores contain clues about the past that can be used to study Earth's climate.

impact effect of one thing on another, such as the effect climate change has on how people live

industrialized nation nation with a lot of industries and high energy consumption

mass transit public transportation system, such as buses or trains, that can carry a lot of people

meteorology study of the climate, weather, and atmosphere

methane greenhouse gas found in natural gas, farming waste, and other waste

molecule group of atoms joined together

nitrous oxide greenhouse gas produced by farming, industry, and the burning of fossil fuels.

ozone form of oxygen found in Earth's upper atmosphere and that is also a greenhouse gas near Earth's surface

photosynthesis process by which plants and algae make food from carbon dioxide, sunlight, and water

power plant place where generators are used to make electricity

renewable able to be replaced

respiration process by which animals break down carbon compounds for energy and which produces carbon dioxide

sustainable able to meet needs without being used up

tax money paid to the government that is used for public costs and services. Taxes can be paid when buying products, such as fuel. They can also be charged as a fee, for example on carbon emissions.

tropical within or having to do with the region of Earth that lies either side of the Equator between the Tropic of Cancer and the Tropic of Capricorn

turbine machine powered by a flow of fluid. The fluid spins the turbine's moving parts to create mechanical energy.

water vapor water in the atmosphere in the form of a gas

yedoma type of permafrost (frozen layer of soil) found in Siberia, a vast region of northern Asia. Like all other soils, yedoma is a carbon sink.

Find Out More

Books

Desonie, Dana. *Climate: Causes and Effects of Climate Change.* New York: Chelsea House Publications, 2008.

Hall, Julie. *A Hot Planet Needs Cool Kids: Understanding Climate Change and What You Can Do About It.* Bainbridge Island, WA: Green Goat Books, 2007.

Harman, Rebecca. *Carbon-Oxygen and Nitrogen Cycles: Respiration, Photosynthesis, and Decomposition.* Chicago: Heinemann Library, 2005.

Johnson, Kirk. *Gas Trees and Car Turds: Kids' Guide to the Roots of Global Warming.* Golden, CO: Fulcrum Publishing, 2007.

Simpson, Kathleen. *Extreme Weather: Science Tackles Global Warming and Climate Change.* Des Moines, IA: National Geographic Children's Books, 2008.

Websites

www.bbc.co.uk/climate/adaptation/
BBC Weather Center—Climate Change—Adaptation
Learn about different ways people can adapt to climate change.

globalwarmingkids.net/web_sites/index.html
Global Warming Kid—Web Sites
Find links to lots of websites about climate change.

www.carbonfootprint.com/calculator.aspx
Carbon Footprint Calculator
Calculate your own carbon footprint.

www.education.noaa.gov/sclimate.html
NOAA Education—Students (Climate Change and Our Planet)
Do your own research, solve puzzles, and find answers about global warming.

www.eia.doe.gov/bookshelf/brochures/greenhouse/Chapter1.htm
EIA - Greenhouse Gases, Climate Change, and Energy
Discover useful facts and statistics about carbon emissions.

Index